A BIG PILE OF BLARNEY!

Baloney is flattery so thick it cannot be true;
blarney is flattery so thin we like it.
— **Monsignor Fulton J Sheen**

First published 2017 by The O'Brien Press Ltd,
12 Terenure Road East, Rathgar, Dublin 6, D06 HD27, Ireland
Tel: +353 1 4923333; Fax: +353 1 4922777
E-mail: books@obrien.ie
Website: www.obrien.ie

The O'Brien Press is a member of Publishing Ireland.

ISBN: 978-1-84717-912-8

Picture credits: p.25: Collection of Euston Hall, Suffolk / Creative
Commons; p.27: Ed Knapen / Creative Commons; pp. 39, 42, 48, 61,
67, 68 and 84 Wikimedia Commons; p.49: Robert Knudsen, White
House / Wikimedia Commons; p.50: Creative Commons; p.55:
Marcel Antonisse/Anefo / Wikimedia Commons; p.58 Bill Smith; p.62
Daryl Mitchell / Creative Commons.

1 3 5 7 8 6 4 2
17 19 21 20 18

Printed and bound in Poland by Białostockie Zakłady Graficzne S.A.
The paper used in this book is produced using pulp from managed
forests.

A Big Pile of Blarney!

Colin Murphy & Brendan O'Reilly

THE O'BRIEN PRESS
DUBLIN

Colin Murphy is the co-author of more than twenty other books, including *The Feckin' Series,* a best-selling collection of humorous books about different aspects of Irish life, and an acclaimed Irish historical novel, *Boycott.* He and Brendan regularly meet to go hillwalking, watch football and talk blarney until the barman kicks them out of the pub. He is married to the gorgeous Gráinne, and they have two grown-up kids, Emmet and Ciára, who are still costing them a fortune, so they'd be grateful if you bought this book to help out!

Brendan O'Reilly is an illustrator and art director in the world of advertising and has also co-authored several books, including *Who's Feckin' Who in Irish History,* which was shortlisted for London's Paddy Power Political Book Awards. And he could even merit an entry himself, being the first man to scale all 407 hills or mountains in Ireland over 500m! His other main ambition in life is to get drunk in every pub in the world named 'The Blarney Stone' (thirty-two down, fifty-six to go). He is married to the lovely Bernie, and they have two children, Vincent and Isobel.

TO THE MEMORY OF FORMER

O'BRIEN PRESS EDITOR

MARY WEBB

CONTENTS

INTRODUCTION

In case you've been living on Mars all your life, you're probably aware that the act of kissing the Blarney Stone supposedly bestows the gift of eloquence on the kisser, commonly known as the gift of the gab, or the gift of blarney.

Now, blarney is often misinterpreted as 'insincere talk designed to cajole or mislead'. As we say in Ireland, that's a ginormous pile of oul' bull! True blarney is designed to entertain, flatter, charm and bring colour and vibrancy to conversation.

The Irish are the world masters at talking. There is no other race on earth who can compete.

WAITER! I ASKED FOR BLARNEY, NOT BALONEY.

You want evidence? Go into any decent Irish pub and listen. We've been talking non-stop for thousands of years. Jaysus, it was the only form of entertainment for centuries and our storytelling ways led directly to the other form of communication at which we are masters – writing.

In fact, 'storytelling' probably better describes Irish verbal intercourse than 'talking'. Because that's what we do all the time. We don't simply relate facts the way other cultures do. We wrap facts in cloaks of silky, colourful words and deliver them

I'VE DISCOVERED WHY YOU'RE TALKING SO MUCH, MR. MURPHY. YOU'VE GOT BLARNEY STONES.

9

with humour and a touch of embellishment, and so entice further inquiry, laughter or some other emotional response.

So, the essence of blarney is not, as many dictionaries would have you believe, to cajole, but to relate everything as though you were telling a tale. OK, the facts might become ever so slightly distorted, but as we say in Ireland, never let the truth get in the way of a good story.

Now, get out there and talk some blarney!

BLARNEY STONE LEGENDS - TAKE YOUR PICK!

According to legend, kissing the Blarney Stone endows the kisser with the gift of gab, eloquence or skill at flattery.

So what's the origin of the stone and how did it come to have its mystical powers? There are almost as many legends as there are steps to Blarney Castle's battlements, and not all of them are clear how the stone came to be imbued with magical powers. But here's a bunch of the most common legends.

APPARENTLY IT'S A COMPLETELY DIFFERENT LEGENDARY STONE WITH MYSTICAL POWERS.

Sweet Dreams

One of the most popular stories involves a fifteenth-century Irish chieftain, Cormac Laidir (meaning 'the strong') MacCarthy, Lord of Muskerry. Cormac had a looming court case and was worried to bejaysus he'd lose. So he prayed to the Irish goddess of love, Clíodhna, who told him to kiss the first stone he saw on his way to court. This might seem like an odd request, but Clíodhna was a right stunner apparently (her very name means 'shapely'), so Cormac was putty in her hands and did as commanded. When he got to court he basically found he had acquired the ability to charm the pants off everyone and the case was dismissed. So he had the stone set into the battlements for evermore.

I PROMISE TO TELL THE BLARNEY, THE WHOLE BLARNEY, AND NOTHING BUT THE BLARNEY.

YE BIBLE

A ROYAL CHARMER

What is considered the most plausible tale concerns a descendent of Cormac Laidir, one Cormac Teige MacCarthy, who was commanded to surrender his rights to Blarney Castle and lands by Queen Elizabeth I. An old woman told Cormac to kiss a particular stone in the parapet, which would bestow the gift of the gab. Whether the old woman bit was true or not, Cormac then apparently so charmed the besieging Earl of Leicester, that the Queen referred to his accounts of Cormac's eloquent chatter as 'all blarney'. Incidentally, Queen Elizabeth never took the castle.

Say the Magic Word

A witch pops up in another legend and the castle grounds actually boasts 'the Witch's Stone', which does look quite hag-like. In this version, one of the MacCarthy clan saves the witch from drowning in Blarney Lough and in gratitude she reveals the location of the magical stone of eloquence in the battlements.

GREAT SCOT

In 1314, yet another, earlier Cormac McCarthy sent four thousand men to help Robert the Bruce of Scotland to disembowel a few thousand English guys at the Battle of Bannockburn. As a thank-you gift, Robert decided to smash off a lump of the Stone of Scone (the Scottish coronation stone) and give it to his new best buddy Cormac. The stone was then brought back to Blarney and set into the walls. How it turns you into a silver-tongued charmer is not explained in this version.

THE STONE OF SCONE

Early Scots pillow fight

PILLOW TALK

There's another Scottish connection in the version
involving one of Ireland's most renowned saints – St
Columba. Back in the sixth century, long after St
Paddy had converted us Micks from pagans to fine
upstanding Christians, St Columba decided he'd do
the same for the heathen Scots. For thirty years
Columba used his eloquence and diplomacy to
convert the Scots. When he died on the island of
Iona, his deathbed pillow was what was to become –
you guessed it – the Blarney Stone. Not very comfy,
you'll agree. Columba's eloquence was transferred
into the stone after he kicked the bucket.

The Old Testament according to the Cork Tourist Board

BIBLICAL TALES

Then there's the biblical version. King Saul ordered his son Jonathan to kill his best friend David (the guy who killed Goliath). Jonathan doesn't want to do this so he tells David to hide behind a particular stone. Leap forward a couple of thousand years and along come the Crusaders, who take this stone as a souvenir and return it to Christendom, and it eventually makes its way into the battlements of Blarney Castle. Sounds totally plausible to us...

Holy Moses!

OK, you want far-fetched? Ever hear the biblical tale of Moses striking a rock in the desert with his staff, from which water magically gushed to quench his people's thirst? Well, guess where the rock he struck ended up? Right, quickly moving on...

No Blarney Here - Just Historical Stuff!

The original fortification was built in the late twelfth century, but was made of wood and tended to catch fire when bad guys shot flaming arrows at it, so occasionally it could get a bit toasty inside.

THIS ISN'T GOOD FOR OUR CARBON FOOTPRINT.

A stone castle was built on the large outcrop of rock in 1210 – so now they could safely throw all sorts of crap down on attackers – literally!

In 1446, Cormac Laidir MacCarthy decided the oul' homestead needed a makeover, demolished the old gaff and built a shiny new castle, which still stands today (well, mostly).

The new castle featured machicolations – openings in the floor around the rim of the battlements that allowed the inhabitants to chuck big rocks, boiling oil, chamber pot contents and all sorts of other nasty stuff down on the heads of besiegers. The famed Blarney Stone is part of this structure, so God only knows what's passed over its surface down the centuries!

The castle withstood many an attack, including attempts by Queen Elizabeth I's boys. In fact, it was finally taken by Cromwellian forces in 1646, the 200th anniversary of its construction, which really screwed up the celebrations.

It was the Anglo-Irish landowner Roger Boyle, also known as Lord Broghill, who finally took Blarney Castle. He despised all Catholics and would have gladly chopped them all into teensy weensy little bits, but when he got inside he discovered they'd all legged it via underground tunnels. Ha ha!

A trouserless Charles II

The castle was given back to the MacCarthy clan in
1661 by Charles II, after the English monarchy was
returned to power in the Restoration. Unfortunately
the MacCarthys didn't have it long, as a couple of
generations later it was seized in the Williamite
Wars and the Brits had it again!

From there, it passed through the Jefferyes family and eventually ended up with the Colthurst family in the nineteenth century. It is the Colthursts who still occupy the estate to this day – nice gaff, m'Lud!

IT'S THE PERFECT STARTER CASTLE FOR A YOUNG COUPLE.

In 1874, the architecturally significant Blarney House was built by Sir James Jefferyes, the former Governor of the City of Cork. The impressive building features pinnacles, crow-stepped gables and myriad turrets with conical roofs, and it overlooks the nearby Blarney Lough, which is really more of a big pond. You can visit that in the summertime.

Blarney Lough. And a cow.

The Jefferyes family also created the nearby Rock Close, a beautiful early eighteenth-century druidic garden complete with huge boulders, yew trees, dolmens, a stone circle and a druid's altar.

The village of Blarney is one of the last so-called 'estate villages' in Ireland — that is, a village built by the estate landlord so that the house and farm workers would have homes nearby.

There is a large boggy area to the east of today's castle, which was once much larger and was reputedly the last habitat for wolves in Cork – but don't worry, the last wolf in Ireland was shot and killed in 1786.

Blarney wolves

Now, that's a fact!

Blarney Castle was strategically sited so that it could overlook two rivers, the Blarney River and the River Martin.

The upper story is believed to have served as a chapel.

IT'S A NICE CASTLE, BUT THE STAIRS ARE A NIGHTMARE

The castle had outer defences that included a curtain wall, some of which survives. The walls are six metres, or eighteen feet, thick in places, so there was never a problem with noise from the neighbours.

IT'S SO QUIET IN HERE.

YES. YOU WOULDN'T THINK THERE'S A SIEGE GOING ON OUTSIDE.

31

The fifteenth-century version of Blarney Castle was built by Cormac Laidir MacCarthy, Lord Muskerry – but it's doubtful whether he ever even lifted a trowel of cement.

The Blarney Stone is a chunk of bluestone that is itself a type of limestone that is as old as the hills, or 350 million years old, if you want to be more accurate.

Pre-Cambrian Blarney stones

The stone is built into the surrounding parapet of Blarney Castle, which is a defensive raised wall that sticks out from the roof and stopped you from getting a spear through your skull.

34

The Blarney stone is situated twenty-six metres, or eighty-five feet, up on the east wall of the battlement, so that's how far you'd fall if you slipped.

The name Blarney comes from the Irish word 'blarna' meaning 'little field'. And by the way, here's how to say 'I kissed the Blarney Stone' in Irish: Phóg mé an chloch Blarnan (pronounced: Foe-g may un cluck Blar-naan)!

Blarney in its purest, agricultural form.

The word blarney has come to mean flattering,
charming, eloquent, witty, seductive, sweet,
bewitching, lovable, colourful, complimentary talk.
Oh, and not forgetting bullshit!

The surviving structure dates from 1446, so people have been slobbering all over it for nearly six centuries!

Oooh, scary. A Blarney Castle stairway.

To get to the Blarney Stone visitors must climb approximately one hundred and twenty steps up a narrow, spiral stairway, so it doesn't help to have claustrophobia, agoraphobia or philematophobia (fear of kissing!).

To kiss the stone you have to lie on your back holding a rail and literally bend over backwards while someone holds your legs. It may not be comfortable but it has stimulated the love life of many a grateful couple.

Before the present-day safeguards were installed, the kiss was performed with genuine risk to life and limb, as kissers were grasped by the ankles and dangled dangerously over the precipice! Lewis's *A Topographical Dictionary of Ireland* (1837) had this to say:

> 'Few, however, venture upon this ceremony [kissing the stone], from the danger in being lowered down to the stone by a rope from an insecure battlement 132 feet high.'

Fancy being kissed four hundred thousand times a year? On the same spot? All of them by complete strangers? Well, have some sympathy for the poor oul' Blarney Stone then.

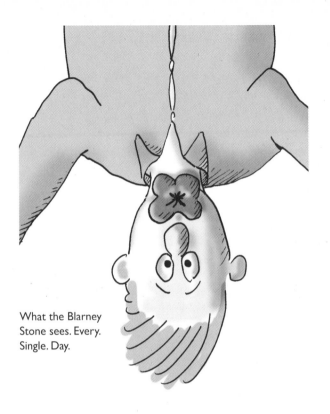

What the Blarney Stone sees. Every. Single. Day.

Nobody knows precisely of course, but it has been estimated that up to fifty million smoochers may have puckered up to the Blarney Stone down the centuries!

43

A FEW FAMOUS KISSERS...

Renowned Scottish author of *Ivanhoe*, *Rob Roy*, *The Lady of the Lake* and a bunch of other literary classics, **Sir Walter Scott** obviously had a way with words. And when someone tried to pull the wool over Sir Walter's eyes he responded: 'All this jargon I answer with corresponding blarney of my own, for have I not licked the black stone of that ancient castle?'

ARE YOU SURE YOU WEREN'T MEANT TO KISS IT RATHER THAN LICK IT, SIR WALTER?

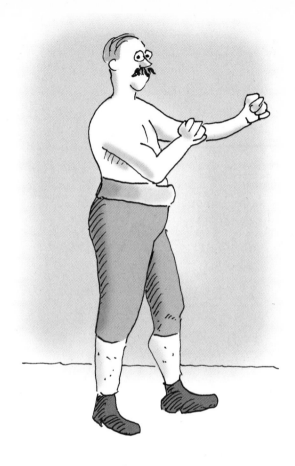

Boxing's first heavyweight champion from 1882
until 1892, and the last bare-knuckle heavyweight
champion, Irish-American **John L Sullivan** was
among the most famous men in the world when he
visited Blarney in 1887. He planted a big smacker on
the Blarney Stone.

A few years later, in 1895, **Milton S Hershey** of
chocolate company fame, dropped by for a kiss.
Now there's a sweet talker if ever there was one.

As your advisor, Mr. President, I should warn that your trip to Ireland could have mellifluous consequences.

No less a figure than US President **William H Taft** (served 1909–1913) said that he 'visited Blarney Castle and kissed the stone with all its mellifluous consequences.' He added, 'If humor be the safety of our race, then it is due largely to the infusion into the American people of the Irish brain.' Fair play te ye, Bill!

Thanks to kissing the Blarney Stone in 1912
when he was British First Lord of the Admiralty,
Winston Churchill went on to become one of the
greatest orators in history!

Churchill after a victorious kissing of the Blarney Stone.

She may not have been First Lady then, but back in the 1950s **Jackie Kennedy** kissed the Blarney Stone and soon after talked her way into JFK's heart.

Presumably Jackie Kennedy was clad appropriately in warm rainproof clothing for her trip to Blarney.

Laurel and Hardy visited in the 1950s, and rumour had it that when Oliver leaned over backwards and saw the huge drop beneath him, he proclaimed to Stan: 'Well, here's another fine mess you've gotten me into!'

Hollywood star **Michael Madsen**, star of *Thelma & Louise*, *Reservoir Dogs* and *Free Willy* has kissed many a leading lady and has also notched up the Blarney Stone.

He's always been blessed with the gift of the gab, but we reckon that when comedian and actor **Billy Connolly** kissed the stone, he was even more garrulous!

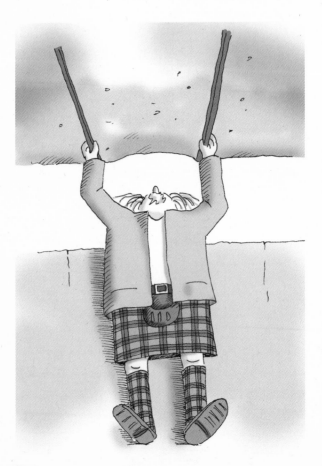

Rock music star **Michael Jackson** was a regular visitor to Cork and naturally his trip to the Blarney Stone was a huge hit with the locals.

The stone presently known as Blarney, was also kissed by the artist formerly known as **Prince**.

OOH, LOOK IT'S
@#**@#
OR WHATEVER THE
SYMBOL WAS?

BLARNEY
CASTLE

Possessing arguably the most famous male lips on earth, **Mick Jagger** has kissed the stone. It seems fitting that a rock legend should kiss a stone legend.

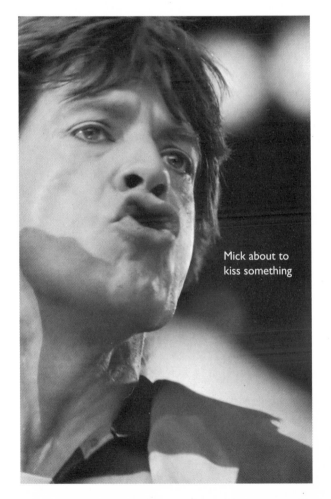

Mick about to kiss something

Pure Blarney Trivia

Priceless

In 1938, a bunch of American businessmen offered
Sir George Colthurst one million dollars – the
equivalent of seventeen million dollars at today's
rates – to take the Blarney Stone on tour in
the USA. George turned the offer down, so he
obviously wasn't short of a few bucks.

Stone Mad

In 2008, British archaeologist Mark Samuels claimed that people had been kissing the wrong stone for over a century and that the actual Blarney Stone is somewhere in another part of the castle. The present castle owners, however, say that is stone mad and that 'the only stone that was ever kissed in Blarney, is the stone people kiss today.'

Archeologists uncover the 'other' Blarney kissing stone.

Pub crawl

There are at least fifty pubs called 'The Blarney Stone' in the following locations: Chicago, Oak Forest (Illinois), Bismarck, West Fargo (North Dakota), Baltimore (Maryland), Berkley, San Diego, El Cajon, Fountain Valley, San Francisco, Orangevale (California), Worthington (Ohio), 8th Avenue, Trinity Place, West 47th Street, 3rd Avenue, 9th Avenue, Syracuse (New York), Virginia Beach, Onancock, Fredericksburg (Virginia), Philadelphia, West Chester (Pennsylvania), Worcester, Dorchester (Massachusetts), St Louis (Missouri), Fort Worth, Dallas, Shamrock (Texas), Venice

The Blarney Stone Pub, Onancock, Virginia, USA.

(Florida), Lanzarote, Torrevieja, Menorca, La Zenia, Alicante (Spain), Panama City (Panama), Vancouver, Killarney (Canada), Amsterdam (Holland), Bordeaux, Dinard (France), Landstuhl (Germany), Dublin (Ireland), Windsor, London (UK), Crete (Greece), Osaka (Japan), Shanghai (China), and Melbourne (Australia). And they're just the ones we're not barred from!

THE HEIGHT OF TERROR

Up until the mid-nineteenth century, anyone who wanted to kiss the Blarney Stone had to be put in a harness and lowered down outside the walls!

IF NOTHING ELSE, IT'LL DO WONDERS FOR OUR DEBATING TEAMS.

STONE DRUNK

There is a monument at the entrance to Texas Tech University topped by a fist-sized piece of rock, which, it is claimed, was taken by an engineering student from the Blarney Stone in Ireland and transported to America. It was unveiled on St Patrick's Day, 1939, after which a large number of beers were downed in celebration. Pure blarney, of course, but a good excuse for a session.

GET REAL!

The World Fair in Chicago in 1893 and the St Louis World Fair of 1904 featured a nearly life-sized replica of Blarney Castle complete with replica Blarney Stone. In fact, the Chicago promoters cheekily claimed the stone was the original until the story was refuted by the real owners.

BLARNEY CASTLE, ON THE MIDWAY.

The D Hotel, Las Vegas

DON'T BET ON THIS

Another so-called chunk of the Blarney Stone is on display in a glamorous hotel in Las Vegas, known simply as 'The D'. Originally Fitzgerald's Hotel, the new owners kept the chunk of rock when they bought the place. Sitting next to a slot machine as girls in skimpy red uniforms and gamblers walk by, the 'Blarney Stone' suspiciously resembles about a billion other lumps of rock you'd find in the desert surrounding the place!

PASS IT ON

In 2009, the travel website TripAdvisor polled its members on the 'world's germiest sites' and guess who won? Yep, the Blarney Stone was triumphant! So there's no better spot in the tourist world to pass on your germs to a complete stranger. For your interest, the runners-up also included another Irish-related site – Oscar Wilde's tomb in Père-Lachaise cemetery in Paris. It's covered in lipstick prints.

HARD LUCK STORIES

According to the Blarney Stone Curse, anyone
removing a stone from the castle or grounds will
be cursed with bad luck. The current owners
frequently receive packages from all over the world
containing stones that had been removed and were
now being returned as the owners had hit rock
bottom. So be warned!

Bucket List It!

TV Channel 'Discovery Travel' lists kissing the Blarney Stone as one of the top ninety-nine things to do before you die.

THAT'S ENTERTAINMENT!
BLARNEY IN BOOKS, MOVIES, TV AND RADIO

SMOOTH TALKIN' WOMAN

Probably the first reference to the Blarney Stone in popular culture is in Irish writer and poet Oliver Goldsmith's classic novel *The Vicar of Wakefield*, written in 1766. The novel features a disreputable character called Lady Blarney, who uses her eloquent tongue to worm her way into the naïve vicar's family.

ONE FOR THE BOOKS

One of the most famous and controversial books of the twentieth century, *Lolita*, by Vladimir Nabokov, features this dialogue between the two main characters:

Lolita: *Have you ever kissed the Blarney Stone?*
Humbert: *No, that's something I never did.*
Lolita: *Boy, I sure wish I could.*

Director of *The European Rest Cure*, Edwin S Porter

THEY DON'T MAKE 'EM LIKE THAT ANYMORE (THANKS BE TO JAYSUS!)

One of the first silent movies, *The European Rest Cure*, featured an unfortunate American tourist on a tour of Europe who has one mishap after the other as he visits various iconic sites (which just happen to be made of plywood and papier mache). He falls off a pyramid, tumbles down the Alps, is mugged in a Pompeii and is dropped from the battlements of Blarney Castle!

Sealed with a Kiss

The year of 1933 saw a movie bearing the title *The Blarney Kiss*, which was about love, sweet-talking and double-crossing in Ireland and London, and which featured the stone at the beginning and end. Hardly a cinematic classic, but good, melodramatic fun by all accounts.

MAKING A SONG AND DANCE

The Blarney Stone's most famous starring role came
in the 1949 movie *Top o' the Morning*, starring Bing
Crosby. Bing plays an insurance investigator who
comes to Ireland to investigate (horror of horrors!)
the theft of the Blarney Stone! Naturally he falls in
love with the local Garda's daughter, recovers the
stone, arrests the bad guy and along the way croons
a whole bunch of songs. It was a huge hit back in
the 1940s.

STOP THE MUSIC!

No less than one of the Fab Four, John Lennon himself, makes mention of the Blarney Stone in his 1972 song, 'Luck of the Irish':

If we could make chains with the morning dew,
The world would be like Galway Bay,
Let's walk over rainbows like leprechauns,
The world would be one big Blarney Stone.

But we'll forgive the great man that one...

Elementary, my dear Blarney

The Adventure of the Blarney Stone was a 1946 radio dramatisation of a Sherlock Holmes story. It involves a man kissing the Blarney Stone who – apparently accidentally – then plummets to his death. Holmes naturally uncovers that a dastardly killer had greased the man's boots!

MAKING WAVES ON THE RADIO
The US state of Michigan has its own Blarney Stone
Broadcasting Company that operates a bunch of
rock and sports stations.

THE SIMPSONS

In the 2009 episode, 'In the Name of the Grandfather', Marge, Lisa and Bart visit Blarney Castle to kiss the stone. Bart sees the opportunity of a prank, sprays his backside grey and sticks it in front the Blarney Stone – and in front of an unfortunate kisser!

THEY HAD THE GIFT OF THE GAB....

Ireland has long been renowned for its writers and storytellers. In fact, per head of population, no country in the world has produced more literary geniuses than our small island. Now, we can't be certain one way or the other whether any of those below kissed the Blarney Stone, but judging by the skill with which they weave their words, we think you'll agree that it's very likely...

JONATHAN SWIFT (1667-1745), IRISH NOVELIST AND SATIRIST

The sight of you is good for sore eyes.

He was a bold man that first ate an oyster.

IT TASTES LIKE PTERODACTYL, BUT FISHIER.

May you live all the days of your life.

There is none so blind as those that will not see.

OLIVER GOLDSMITH (1728-1774),
IRISH NOVELIST AND POET

She wears her clothes as if they were thrown on to her with a pitchfork.

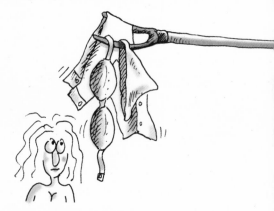

For he who fights and runs away
May live to fight another day,
But he who is in battle slain
Can never rise and fight again.

And still they gazed and still the wonder grew, that one small head could carry all that he knew.
The loud laugh that spoke the vacant mind.

JOHN MAHAFFY (1839-1919),
IRISH POLYMATH AND SCHOLAR

An Irish atheist is one who wishes to God he could believe in God.

DEAR GOD, I KNOW YOU'RE NOT THERE, BUT ON THE REMOTE OFF-CHANCE...

(On hearing that the incumbent of the coveted post of Provost of Trinity College was ill.)
Nothing trivial, I hope?

In Ireland the inevitable never happens and the unexpected constantly occurs.

(On being asked, by a women's rights advocate, what the difference was between a man and a woman.)
I can't conceive.

Oscar Wilde (1854-1900), Irish playwright, novelist and poet

I can resist everything except temptation.

Work is the curse of the drinking classes.

The only thing worse than being talked about is not being talked about.

Biography lends to death a new terror.

(On being questioned at New York's Customs Hall.) I have nothing to declare except my genius.

The play was a great success, but the audience was a disaster.

The English country gentleman galloping after a fox — the unspeakable in full pursuit of the uneatable.

Nothing succeeds like excess.

True friends stab you in the front.

GEORGE BERNARD SHAW (1856-1950),
IRISH PLAYWRIGHT

I often quote myself. It adds spice to my conversations.

There are two tragedies in life. One is not to get your heart's desire. The other is to get it.

Youth is a wonderful thing. What a crime to waste it on children.

If all economists were laid end to end, they would not reach a conclusion.

Dancing: the vertical expression of a horizontal desire.

A drama critic is a man who leaves no turn unstoned.

Better never than late.

A life making mistakes is not only more honourable, but more useful than a life spent doing nothing at all.

William Butler Yeats (1865-1939), Irish poet

Education is not the filling of a pail, but rather the lighting of a fire.

There are no strangers here; only friends you haven't yet met.

Being Irish, he had an abiding sense of tragedy, which sustained him through temporary periods of joy.

Life is a long preparation for something that never happens.

But I, being poor, have only my dreams; I have
spread my dreams beneath your feet; Tread softly
because you tread on my dreams.

JAMES CONNOLLY (1868-1910),
IRISH REPUBLICAN LEADER

The worker is the slave of capitalist society, the
female worker is the slave of that slave.

Apostles of freedom are ever idolised when dead, but
crucified when alive.

SEAN O'CASEY (1880-1954),
IRISH PLAYWRIGHT

Laughter is wine for the soul.

It's my rule never to lose me temper 'til it would be
detrimental to keep it.

Money does not make you happy but it quiets the
nerves.

No man is so old as to believe he cannot live one
more year.

There's no reason to bring religion into it. I think
we ought to have as great a regard for religion as
we can, so as to keep it out of as many things as
possible.

All the world's a stage and most of us are desperately unrehearsed.

HE THINKS THAT ALL OF LIFE'S A STAGE...

BUS STOP

John Fitzgerald Kennedy (1917-1963), Irish-American US President

Forgive your enemies, but never forget their names.

Let us never negotiate out of fear. But let us never fear to negotiate.

Mankind must put an end to war before war puts an end to mankind.

A man may die, nations may rise and fall, but an idea lives on.

Spike Milligan (1918-2002),
Irish comedian, writer and actor

Contraceptives should be used on every conceivable occasion.

I'm not afraid of dying I just don't want to be there when it happens.

I have the body of an eighteen-year-old. I keep it in the fridge.

Is there anything worn under the kilt? No, it's all in perfect working order.

How long was I in the army? Five foot eleven.

All I ask is a chance to prove that money can't make me happy.

Brendan Behan (1923-1964),
Irish playwright and novelist

The big difference between sex for money and sex for free is that sex for money usually costs a lot less.

I was court-martialled in my absence, and sentenced to death in my absence, so I said they could shoot me in my absence.

There is no such thing as bad publicity, except your own obituary.

I saw a sign that said 'Drink Canada Dry'. So I did.

I only take drink on two occasions – when I'm thirsty and when I'm not.

Critics are like eunuchs in a harem: they know how it's done, they've seen it done every day, but they're unable to do it themselves.

I am a drinker with writing problems.

GEORGE BEST (1946-2005),
NORTHERN IRISH PROFESSIONAL FOOTBALLER

In 1969 I gave up women and alcohol and it was the worst twenty minutes of my life.

(On having a liver transplant.) I was in for ten hours and had forty pints – beating my previous record by twenty minutes.

I always had a reputation for going missing... Miss England, Miss United Kingdom, Miss World...

I blew hundreds of thousands of pounds on women and drinking – the rest I squandered.

BLARNEY IN QUOTATION AND RHYME

Blarney is something more than mere flattery. It is flattery sweetened by humour and flavoured by wit. Those who mix with Irish folk have many examples of it in their everyday experience.
JOHN O'CONNOR POWER (1846-1919),
FENIAN POLITICIAN

MINE'S A LARGE FLATTERY WITH A DOLLOP OF WIT AND A TWIST OF HUMOUR.

A cajoling tongue

If anyone kisses the Blarney Stone, he will ever after have a cajoling tongue and the art of flattery, or of telling fibs with unblushing effrontery.
SAMUEL LEWIS (1782-1865), PUBLISHER

'Tis there's the stone that whoever kisses
He never misses to grow eloquent;
'Tis he may clamber to a lady's chamber,
Or become a member of Parliament.
A noble spouter he'll sure turn out, or
An out and outer to be let alone;
Don't try to hinder him, or to bewilder him,
For he is a pilgrim from the Blarney stone.
FRANCIS SYLVESTER MAHONY (1804-1866),
IRISH HUMORIST

Blarney, Blarney! I'll hear no more of this Blarney!
QUEEN ELIZABETH I (1533-1603), ATTRIBUTED

Baloney is when you tell a 50-year old woman that she looks 18. Blarney is when you ask a woman how old she is, because you want to know at what age women are most beautiful.
FULTON J SHEEN (1895-1979),
AMERICAN CLERIC

When you've kissed the Blarney Stone you'll have the ability to take both sides of an argument at the same time – and win!
ANONYMOUS

GENUINE IRISH BLARNEY

Kissed the Blarney Stone or not, these few nuggets of witty and wise Irish blarney from generations past will always come in handy in a conversation or a debate!

'Tis better to spend money like there's no tomorrow than to spend tonight like there's no money!

May you have the hindsight to know where you've been, the foresight to know where you are going, and the insight to know when you have gone too far.

A good laugh and a long sleep are the two best cures.

You'll never plough a field by turning it over in your mind.

If you want praise, die. If you want blame, marry.

There's nothing better than warm words on a cold night.

A girl is a daughter all her life but a boy is a son until he takes a wife.

No matter how many rooms you have in your house you can only sleep in the one bed.

You've got to do your own growing, no matter how tall your father was.

There are only two kinds of people in the world, the Irish and those who wish they were.

It is often that a person's mouth broke his nose.

May you live as long as you want,
And never want as long as you live.

May you always have a clean shirt, a clear conscience, and enough coins in your pocket to buy a pint!

May you get all your wishes but one, so that you will always have something to strive for!

May you live to be a hundred years, with one extra year to repent.

Forgetting a debt doesn't mean it's paid.

If you come up in this world be sure not to go down in the next.

Where the tongue slips, it speaks the truth.

May the roof above you never fall in, and those gathered beneath it never fall out.

As you slide down the banister of life, may the splinters never point the wrong way.

May misfortune follow you the rest of your life, and never catch up.

Lose an hour in the morning and you'll be looking for it all day.

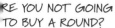

Better be sparing at first than at last.

Pity him who makes an opinion a certainty.

May your home always be too small to hold all your friends.

Who keeps his tongue keeps his friends.

May you have food and raiment, a soft pillow for your head. May you be forty years in heaven before the devil knows you're dead.

A cottage with plenty of food is better than a hungry castle.

Take the world nice and easy, and the world will take you the same.

A Blarney joke!

A group of tourists were visiting Ireland and one of the women in the group was a terrible one for complaining. Everything was wrong according to her: the food, the accommodation, the weather, the prices. And all the others in the group were fed up listening to her whinging.

Next stop on their tour was Blarney Castle in County Cork.

'If you kiss the Blarney Stone,' the guide said, 'you will have good luck and eloquence for the rest of your days. Unfortunately, it's being cleaned today so sadly no one will be able to kiss it. Perhaps you can all come back tomorrow.'

'We can't come back tomorrow,' snapped the bad-tempered woman. 'I'm so disappointed. This whole tour is terrible. I'm sick of everything!'

'Well now,' the guide, said patiently, 'it is said that if you kiss someone who has kissed the stone, you'll have the same good luck and eloquence.' 'And I suppose you've kissed the stone?' the woman snapped sarcastically. 'No, ma'am,' replied the guide, 'but I have sat on it.'

Slán go fóill

(Translation: 'Bye for now', pronounced 'Slaun guh foe-ill'.)

Let's say farewell with an Irish blarney-like blessing!

May the road rise up to meet you.
May the wind be always at your back.
May the sun shine warm upon your face,
and rains fall soft upon your fields.
And until we meet again,
May God hold you in the palm of His hand.